A+

A GIFT FOR:

Mrs. Morales

FROM:

Suzie Hernandez

DATE:

12/17/04

Crazy About My Teacher

BARBOUR
PUBLISHING

Crazy About My Teacher

"THE WISE PERSON
MAKES LEARNING
A JOY."

PROVERBS 15:2

I'M CRAZY ABOUT MY TEACHER
BECAUSE SHE CARES ENOUGH
TO ASK IF MY SICK DOG IS OKAY.

I'M CRAZY ABOUT MY TEACHER BECAUSE SHE IS IN A GREAT MOOD EVERY MORNING WHEN SHE ARRIVES AT SCHOOL.

I'M CRAZY ABOUT MY TEACHER BECAUSE SHE IS SO PATIENT AND UNDERSTANDS THAT KIDS GET A LITTLE ROWDY SOME DAYS.

I hope Mrs. ~~Smith~~ Morales doesn't come back soon.

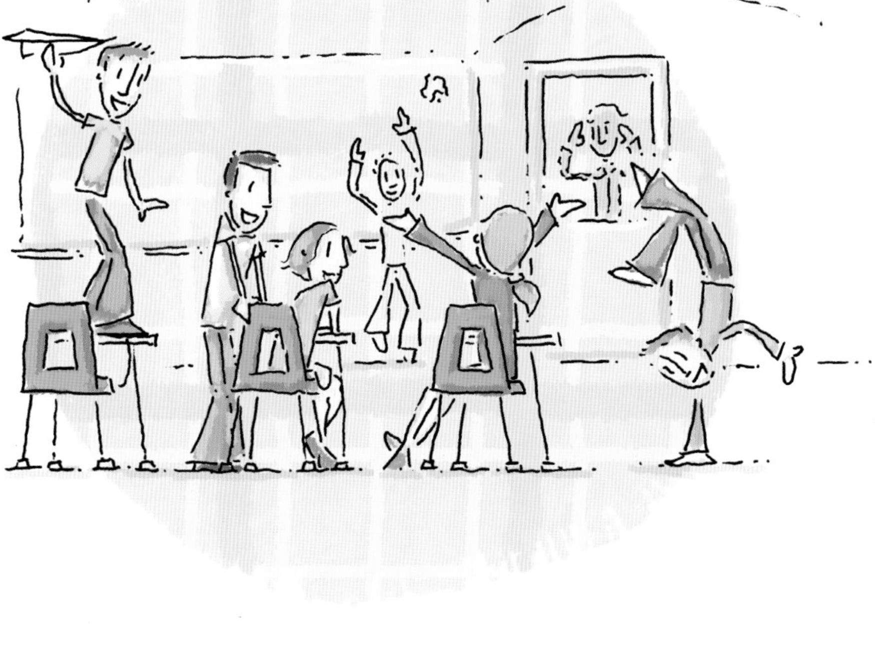

I'M CRAZY ABOUT MY TEACHER
BECAUSE SHE IS CONCERNED THAT
I GET A GOOD NIGHT'S SLEEP.

I'M CRAZY ABOUT MY TEACHER
BECAUSE SHE REALLY IS
ABLE TO SEE BEHIND HER.

I'M CRAZY ABOUT MY TEACHER
BECAUSE SHE IS A WORLD-CLASS
MULTITASKER.

I'M CRAZY ABOUT MY TEACHER
BECAUSE SHE GETS DISTRACTED
SOMETIMES, TOO.

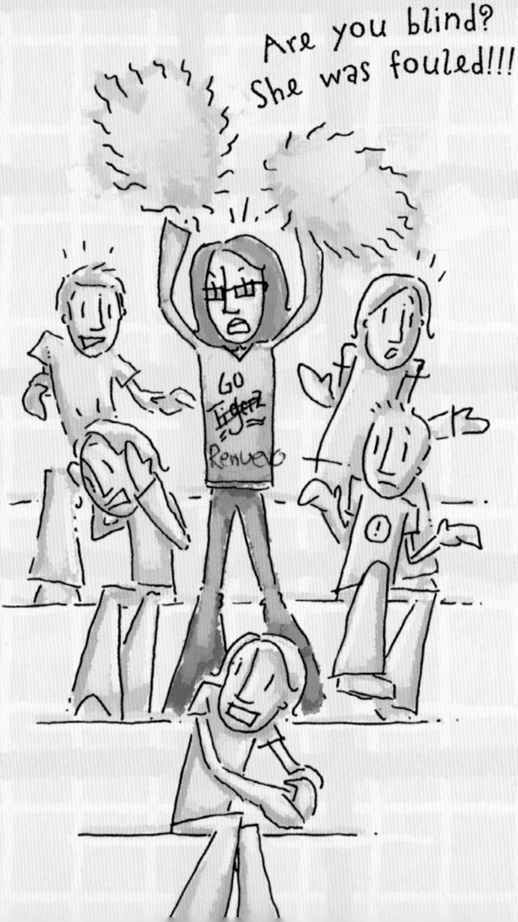
Are you blind?
She was fouled!!!
GO

I'M CRAZY ABOUT MY TEACHER
BECAUSE SHE MODELS SCHOOL SPIRIT.

I'M CRAZY ABOUT MY TEACHER
BECAUSE SHE IS INTERESTED
IN WHAT'S ON MY MIND.

Come on baby. . .let's do the twist!

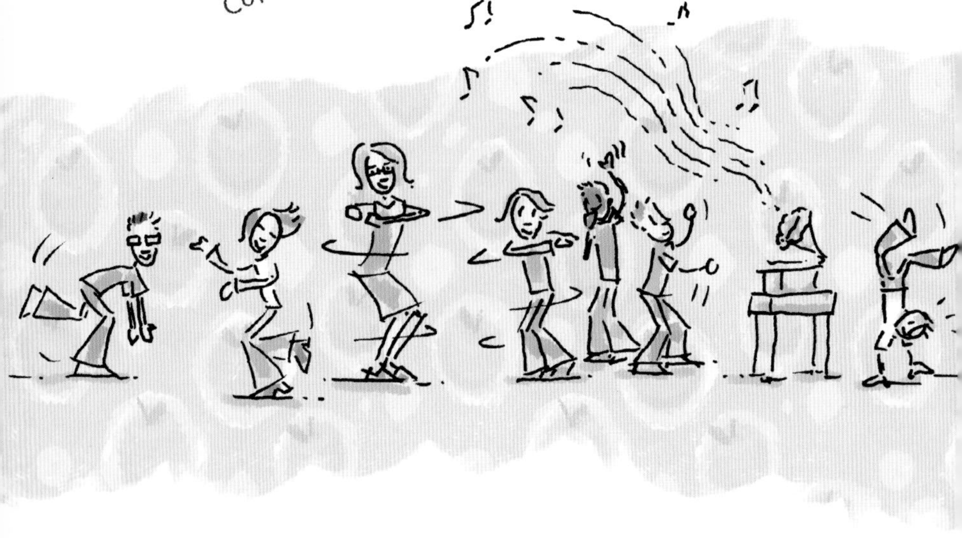

I'M CRAZY ABOUT MY TEACHER
BECAUSE SHE MAKES
MUSIC CLASS LOTS OF FUN.

I'M CRAZY ABOUT MY TEACHER
BECAUSE SHE ACTS JUST LIKE ONE OF US.

I'M CRAZY ABOUT MY TEACHER
BECAUSE SHE KNOWS HOW IMPORTANT
MY SOCIAL LIFE IS ON WEEKENDS.

I'M CRAZY ABOUT MY TEACHER
BECAUSE SHE IS SO WELL-READ.

I'M CRAZY ABOUT MY TEACHER BECAUSE I'M SURE SHE MISSES US TERRIBLY OVER SUMMER VACATION.

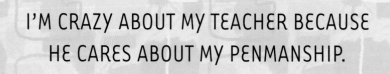

I'M CRAZY ABOUT MY TEACHER BECAUSE
HE CARES ABOUT MY PENMANSHIP.

will not interrupt while others are talking
will not interrupt while others are talking
will not interru hile others are talking
will not interru hile
Hi, BEN!!!!

I'M CRAZY ABOUT MY TEACHER BECAUSE SHE MAKES STORY TIME A BLAST.

I'M CRAZY ABOUT MY TEACHER
BECAUSE SHE IS GREAT AT
DECORATING HER ROOM.

I'M CRAZY ABOUT MY TEACHER
BECAUSE SHE GETS AS EXCITED ABOUT
CHRISTMAS BREAK AS ~~HIS~~ HER STUDENTS.

I'M CRAZY ABOUT MY TEACHER
BECAUSE SHE LIKES TO
CELEBRATE BIRTHDAYS, TOO.

I'M CRAZY ABOUT MY TEACHER
BECAUSE SHE NEVER FORGETS NAMES.

I'M CRAZY ABOUT MY TEACHER
BECAUSE SHE KNOWS HOW TO
MOTIVATE US TO LEARN.

I guess I already mentioned that this is going to be on tomorrow's test and worth 60% of your grade.

I'M CRAZY ABOUT MY TEACHER
BECAUSE SHE SEEMS TO
HAVE UNLIMITED ENERGY.

I'M CRAZY ABOUT MY TEACHER
BECAUSE SHE GETS THE
RAINY DAY BLUES, TOO.

I'M CRAZY ABOUT MY TEACHER
BECAUSE SHE ENCOURAGES US
TO GIVE OUR VERY BEST.

I'M CRAZY ABOUT MY TEACHER
BECAUSE SHE TELLS THE FUNNIEST JOKES.
(Sometimes) :)

And then the lion
yells to the monkey...

I'M CRAZY ABOUT MY TEACHER
BECAUSE SHE TEACHES US
HOW TO SPEAK PROPERLY.

I'M CRAZY ABOUT MY TEACHER
BECAUSE I KNOW SHE'S JUST
A REGULAR PERSON, TOO.

I'M CRAZY ABOUT MY TEACHER
BECAUSE HER CLASSROOM IS
FULL OF WONDERFUL SCENTS.

I'M CRAZY ABOUT MY TEACHER
BECAUSE SHE AGREES WITH US
ON THE TASTE OF CAFETERIA FOOD

(EVEN IF SHE WON'T ADMIT IT).

I'M CRAZY ABOUT MY TEACHER
BECAUSE SHE IS FAMOUS
EVERYWHERE SHE GOES.

I'M CRAZY ABOUT MY TEACHER BECAUSE
SHE HAS THE WISDOM OF SOLOMON.

Then Long John Silver said, "Yo, ho, ho..."

I'M CRAZY ABOUT MY TEACHER
BECAUSE SHE MAKES LEARNING FUN.

I'M CRAZY ABOUT MY TEACHER
BECAUSE AFTER ALL OUR HARD WORK
SOMETIMES SHE LETS US RELAX
FOR THE AFTERNOON.

I'M CRAZY ABOUT MY TEACHER
BECAUSE HE DOES HOMEWORK, TOO,
AND HE HAS THE BIGGEST BACKPACK
IN OUR CLASS.

I'M CRAZY ABOUT MY TEACHER
BECAUSE SHE LOVES GETTING
GIFTS FROM HER FAVORITE STUDENT.

I'M CRAZY ABOUT MY TEACHER
BECAUSE SHE KNOWS KIDS NEED
SECOND CHANCES SOMETIMES.

I'M CRAZY ABOUT MY TEACHER
BECAUSE SHE HELPS US RESPECT
EACH OTHER AND ALL LIVING THINGS.

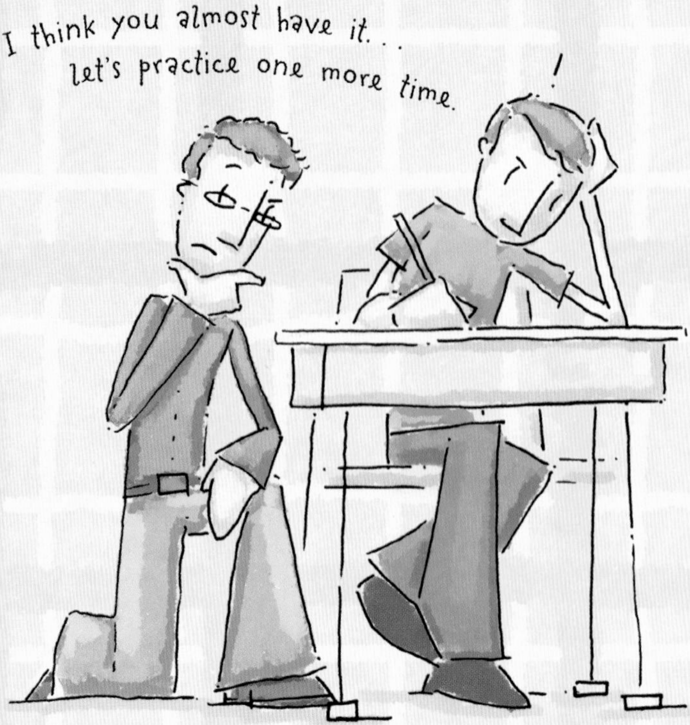
I think you almost have it. . .
let's practice one more time.
!

I'M CRAZY ABOUT MY TEACHER
BECAUSE SHE REALLY DOES
CARE ABOUT HOW WELL I DO.

I'M CRAZY ABOUT MY TEACHER
BECAUSE SHE TEACHES MORE
THAN JUST BOOK KNOWLEDGE.

And the reason we show
respect to our country is. . .

I'M CRAZY ABOUT MY TEACHER
BECAUSE SHE KNOWS THAT SOMETIMES
EVEN TEACHERS NEED EXTRA HELP.

I'M CRAZY ABOUT MY TEACHER
BECAUSE SHE ALWAYS KNOWS
THE RIGHT THING TO SAY.

It's amazing what so many of these
children go on to accomplish and become...

I'M CRAZY ABOUT MY TEACHER
BECAUSE EVEN IF SHE ISN'T RICH,
MY MOM SAYS SHE IS A GREAT INVESTOR.

I'M CRAZY ABOUT MY TEACHER
BECAUSE SHE IS CRAZY ABOUT ME.

I'M CRAZY ABOUT MY TEACHER
BECAUSE HER STUDENTS
GIVE HER STRAIGHT A'S.

I'M CRAZY ABOUT MY TEACHER
BECAUSE HE IS COMMITTED
TO BEING A GREAT TEACHER.

I'M CRAZY ABOUT MY TEACHER
BECAUSE SHE MAKES
MY HEART THANKFUL.

EVERY TIME
I THINK OF YOU,
I GIVE THANKS
TO MY GOD.
PHILIPPIANS 1:3